IMAGES OF WAR

GERMAN MOTORCYCLES AT WAR 1939–1945

RARE PHOTOGRAPHS FROM WARTIME ARCHIVES

Ian Baxter

Pen & Sword
MILITARY

First published in Great Britain in 2024 by
PEN & SWORD MILITARY
an imprint of Pen & Sword Books Ltd
Yorkshire – Philadelphia

ISBN 978-1-03610-056-8

A CIP catalogue record for this book is available from the British Library.

Typeset by Concept, Huddersfield HD4 5JL.
Printed and bound in England by CPI Group (UK) Ltd, Croydon CR0 4YY.

MIX
Paper | Supporting responsible forestry
FSC® C013604

Pen & Sword Books Limited incorporates the imprints of After the Battle, Atlas, Archaeology, Aviation, Discovery, Family History, Fiction, History, Maritime, Military, Military Classics, Politics, Select, Transport, True Crime, Air World, Frontline Publishing, Leo Cooper, Remember When, Seaforth Publishing, The Praetorian Press, Wharncliffe Local History, Wharncliffe Transport, Wharncliffe True Crime and White Owl.

For a complete list of Pen & Sword titles please contact
PEN & SWORD BOOKS LTD
47 Church Street, Barnsley, South Yorkshire, S70 2AS, England
E-mail: enquiries@pen-and-sword.co.uk
Website: www.pen-and-sword.co.uk
or
PEN & SWORD BOOKS
1950 Lawrence Rd, Havertown, PA 19083, USA
E-mail: uspen-and-sword@casematepublishers.com
Website: www.penandswordbooks.com

Contents

About the Author

Ian Baxter is a military historian who specialises in German twentieth-century military history. He has written more than fifty books including *Poland – The Eighteen Day Victory March, Panzers in North Africa, The Ardennes Offensive, The Western Campaign, The 12th SS Panzer-Division Hitlerjugend, The Waffen-SS on the Western Front, The Waffen-SS on the Eastern Front, The Red Army at Stalingrad, Elite German Forces of World War II, Armoured Warfare, German Tanks of War, Blitzkrieg, Panzer-Divisions at War 1939–1945, Hitler's Panzers, German Armoured Vehicles of World War Two, Last Two Years of the Waffen-SS at War, German Soldier Uniforms and Insignia, German Guns of the Third Reich, Defeat to Retreat: The Last Years of the German Army at War 1943–45, Operation Bagration – the Destruction of Army Group Centre, German Guns of the Third Reich, Rommel and the Afrika Korps, U-Boat War*, and most recently, *The Sixth Army and the Road to Stalingrad.* He has written over a hundred articles including 'Last days of Hitler', 'Wolf's Lair', 'The Story of the V1 and V2 Rocket Programme', 'Secret Aircraft of World War Two', 'Rommel at Tobruk', 'Hitler's War with his Generals', 'Secret British Plans to Assassinate Hitler', 'The SS at Arnhem', 'Hitlerjugend', 'Battle of Caen 1944', 'Gebirgsjäger at War', 'Panzer Crews', 'Hitlerjugend Guerrillas', 'Last Battles in the East', 'The Battle of Berlin', and many more. He has also reviewed numerous military studies for publication, supplied thousands of photographs and important documents to various publishers and film production companies worldwide, and lectures to various schools, colleges and universities throughout the United Kingdom and the Republic of Ireland.

Introduction

The motorcycle became part of the arsenal of the German war machine. It was an important component in the tactics of blitzkrieg. France and later Russia suffered at the hands of the Germans in this type of war and motorcycles made a significant impact in these campaigns, at least in the early stages of the German offensive.

The German military perfected the use of the motorcycle and employed the largest number of bikes for their operations, the troops becoming known as the *Kradschützen Truppen*. They were motorized, lightly armed and highly mobile infantry units of the Wehrmacht, Waffen-SS and Luftwaffe.

The *Kradschützen Truppen* were used in a variety of roles including patrolling, intelligence gathering, and police duties in occupied Europe. Motorcyclists could be found in every unit of an infantry and panzer division, especially during the early part of the war. They were even incorporated into the divisional staffs, which included a motorcycle messenger platoon. Their versatility enabled them to survey enemy positions until they encountered enemy fire and then to return swiftly with important data and vital information relating to the location and strength of the enemy.

By 1938 some 200,000 motorcycles were made each year in Germany and its occupied territories. German industry produced an array of bikes for use by the army, principal makes including BMW, DKW, NSU, Triumph, Victoria, and Zündapp.

Additionally, sidecar combinations were often mounted with an MG34/42 machine gun for local defence and for use in battle. This made the bike a very effective weapon.

This book tells the story of the *Kradschützen Truppen* at war and how they became an important part of operations in all the theatres of war. It shows how they were moulded into a rapid mobile assault and reconnaissance force that played an integral part in the German Blitzkrieg successes of 1939–40. By 1943 however, the development of *Kampfgruppen*, panzer grenadier regiments and armoured halftracks, meant that large formations of lightly armed *Kradschützen Truppen* became obsolete, and the soldiers were transferred to other services. For the remainder of the war the motorcycles would be relegated to support roles such as despatch riders, messengers and light reconnaissance.

Chapter One

Origins of the *Kradschützen Truppen*

Through the mid-to-late 1930s the manufacture of German motorcycles increased drastically as the Nazi war machine grew in preparation for conflict. Designers and manufacturers worked to develop the motorcycle as an instrument of offensive warfare, perhaps more than in any other country in the world. Initially, when the motorcycle first entered military service it was used to protect motorcades for dignitaries, Nazi officials, and high ranking military officers as well as for policing measures, such as crowd control and keeping order during ceremonies and rallies. Motorcycles were also used for Hitler's personal security, often forming part of the Führer's escort for additional support and protection. Hitler frequently travelled in his open tourer through the streets of 'liberated' cities such as Prague and other annexed towns and cities. Security found that the crowds were controlled more easily in the Sudeten areas, where motorcycle and armoured support was often more relaxed.

Although Prague had a certain number of supporters of German occupation, security in the capital was nonetheless increased during Hitler's tour in March 1939. His security detail comprised two groups of well armed cars, protected by the *Führer-Begleit-Bataillon*. These vehicles were further supported by a squad of five soldiers on motorcycles and by two armed reconnaissance vehicles.

The versatility of the motorcycle for personal security and policing measures made the machine an ideal component in a military role. Its speed and manoeuvrability allowed it to become an integral part of battlefield operations. It could be used in reconnaissance roles, major tasks such as mopping-up enemy areas and employment as an advance guard, for surprise attacks against an enemy's flanks and rear, as well as in pursuit of withdrawing enemy formations and units.

A wide variety of machines were deployed for these tasks, including adapted civilian motorcycles as well as purpose-built military models. By 1938, approximately 200,000 motorcycles were manufactured annually in Germany. Among the various types produced were the BMW R12 and R17, both flat-twin engine motorcycles made by BMW Motorrad from 1935 to 1942. The BMW R75, built in 1938, was a highly effective machine complete with sidecar combination. It featured an integral two-wheel drive design, with drive shafts to both its rear wheel and the third sidecar wheel, from a locking differential, as well as a transfer case, which gave it both road and off-road gear ratios, through which all forward and reverse gears worked. Because of its unique design the bike was highly manoeuvrable and capable of negotiating almost all types of road and also had off-road capability.

Another vehicle to enter service in the late 1930s was the Zündapp KS600. The bike was often coupled with a Steib sidecar, the BW38 (Beiwagen 1938). The BW38, fitted with the B1 (Boot no. 1) sidecar body, was produced between 1938 and 1941 and supplied exclusively to the Wehrmacht. Many of the motorcycles were produced with additional sidecars. Often armed with an MG34 for close support, these light vehicles were used extensively for reconnaissance and supporting infantry columns. Unlike similar motorcycles in other countries, the majority of German sidecars had powered wheels, enabling them to traverse difficult terrain more easily. In all units of the Wehrmacht the motorcycle became the favoured transportation choice, especially for relaying messages to the front, reconnaissance duties, and assisting in closing the wide distances between mobile forward units. The motorcyclists became known as the *Kradschützen Truppen*. They were motorized, lightly armed and highly mobile infantry units of the Wehrmacht and Waffen-SS, and were often incorporated into the panzer divisions. *Kradschützen* units were also trained as a rapid mobile assault and reconnaissance force and would play an integral part in the German Blitzkrieg successes of 1939–40.

A photograph taken in the late 1930s showing motorcycle maintenance at a workshop making minor mechanical adjustments to the BMW motorcycle.

Wehrmacht dispatch riders pose for the camera at their home station with their single and sidecar motorcycle combinations.

During a parade at a home Wehrmacht station motorcycle combinations display their versatility and speed across the parade ground.

(**Above**) A motorcyclist is wearing the double-breasted rubberized motorcycle coat and aviator goggles over his M35 steel helmet.

(**Opposite, above**) A group of stationary motorcycle combination troops in a German urbanized area receiving much attention from young children.

(**Opposite, below**) A posed photograph showing single and motorcycle combinations in a German town in the late 1930s. All of the Wehrmacht *Truppen* wear the double-breasted rubberized motorcycle coat and aviator goggles either around their neck or positioned on their M35 steel helmets.

This photograph was more than likely taken during Anschluss with the Sudetenland in March 1938. It shows a column of light armoured vehicles and a single motorcycle moving along a road.

A motorcyclist can be seen making minor mechanical adjustments out in the field to his BMW R75 motorcycle. The R75 were powered by a 750cc side valve engine, which was based on the R71 engine. However it was quickly found necessary to design an all-new OHV 750cc engine for the R75 unit.

Two good photographs showing motorcyclists clad in their familiar double-breasted rubberized motorcycle coats during an exercise. Apart from the greatcoat that was worn almost universally among troops of the German Army, especially during the first half of the war, another form of protective clothing was issued solely to members of motorcycle units and individual motorcyclists – the waterproof coat. This double-breasted garment was made of cotton twill coated with rubber, with watertight seams, and was worn over the service uniform. The coat was loose-fitting and the ends could easily be gathered in around the wearer's legs and buttoned into position, to allow easier and safer movement whilst riding the motorcycle.

(**Above**) A motorcyclist poses for the camera next to his machine, probably in 1938. He wears his motorcycle rubberized coat, which was grey-green in colour and had a woollen field-grey material collar and large pockets. The motorcyclist normally wore the coat together with army canvas and leather issue gloves or mittens. Ordinary leather army boots were often worn.

(**Opposite, above**) During a parade a motorcycle combination drives along, passing lines of civilians at the roadside.

(**Opposite, below**) A motorcyclist complete with combination smiles for the camera. The bike has been adorned with flowers, which probably indicates this photo was taken in March 1938 during Anschluss with Austria. Thousands of Sudeten Germans filled the roads, littering villages and towns with flowers and greeting soldiers with glasses of schnapps.

This photograph was taken at the Austrian border during Anschluss. Wehrmacht soldiers tuck into some rations next to a car. Note the stationary motorcycle. One of the soldiers has taken off his black leather infantryman's belt complete with Karbiner 98K ammunition pouches which sit on the rear of the machine.

Taken during the late 1930s showing motorcyclists wearing black armoured uniforms complete with black Wehrmacht beret. The black panzer beret was the first item of headgear issued to be worn with the special panzer uniform. It was soon replaced during the winter of 1939/40 for the black field cap, identical to that of the army field grey M1938 field cap.

Chapter Two

Blitzkrieg

When the first panzer divisions were formed by the German Army in the 1930s, their infantry component was given the title of *Schützen*. They were fully motorized and were able to move to any area of operation without the need for additional transport. An important element of a *Schützen* and a panzer division were the *Kradschützen*, or motorcycle rifle units. The Wehrmacht was a heavy user of motorcycles, both solo bikes and those fitted with sidecar combinations. The use of motorcycles in fast moving panzer divisions gave the German Army a quick and cost-effective means to motorize their infantry units. A typical *Schützen* unit in 1939 comprised three motorcycle rifle companies, using sidecar combinations carrying both light and heavy MG34 machine guns. The third motorcycle company was often denoted the MG Company and was armed with eight *Kradschützen Truppen* all carrying heavy machine guns.

In total there were some forty-one *Kradschützen Truppen*. However, there were some structural variations. When Germany unleashed its war against Poland in September 1939, the 1st, 2nd and 3rd Panzer Divisions each had a *Kradschützen* battalion comprising two motorcycle rifle companies, one motorcycle MG Company and one heavy company. The 4th Panzer Division, however, was comprised of one *Schützen* Regiment containing one motorcycle platoon. Its battalion headquarters had one motorcycle, two motorized in II battalion, and all motorized in I battalion. The 5th Panzer Division had two *Schützen* regiments each with a motorcycle platoon. Its battalion headquarters had one motorcycle battalion. The 6th and 8th Panzer Divisions had one *Kradschützen* battalion comprising three motorcycle rifle companies. The 7th Panzer Division also had one *Kradschützen* battalion but comprising two motorcycle rifle companies. The 9th and 10th Panzer Divisions each had two *Schützen* regiments, each containing a motorcycle platoon. The 10th also had one motorcycle in the battalion headquarters.

In all the motorcycle MG Companies, the MG platoons were carried on motorcycle combinations. Some of the *Kradschützen* were paired with armoured car battalions to form a reconnaissance regiment. In the 9th Panzer Division for instance, the division had quite a sizeable *Kradschützen* battalion which was paired with an armoured battalion to form the 9th Reconnaissance Regiment.

Most of the panzer divisions were comprised of a company headquarters, a heavy machine gun group, three rifle platoons and the company trains. The motorcycle rifle platoon had a headquarters, three rifle squads and a 5cm mortar troop. It comprised thirty-eight men, distributed across two cars and thirteen motorcycles, eleven of which were fitted with a sidecar. A typical *Kradschützen* squad had an NCO and eight men, with three motorcycle combinations. Each machine gun had to carry three men: the driver, a passenger on the pillion seat behind him, and another in the sidecar combination. Within the squad there were three men chosen as drivers and four as numbers for the squad's single light machine gun. This left one of the *Truppen* as a rifleman and the squad leader. Two of the light machine-gun team were armed with side pistols and the rest of the squad were armed with rifles.

At platoon headquarters, however, were an officer, three messengers, two of whom were solo motorcyclists, and a stretcher-bearer. There were two cars, one a Kfz.11 light car and the other a Kfz.15. Supporting the platoon was a three-man 5cm mortar troop including two motorcycle combinations, each with a driver.

The heavy machine-gun group contained two guns and four motorcycle combinations. The *Kradschützen* company headquarters had six messengers dispersed among three motorcycles.

For the invasion of Poland the *Kradschützen Truppen* were an important component and a vital instrument in the Wehrmacht's blitzkrieg tactics. During operations through Poland the motorcycle troops were used as couriers or for scouting and were also part of teams of tank hunters. They supported the divisions of rifle troops and were escorts for the military police. The bikes had other uses such as patrolling, intelligence gathering, and messaging. The summer weeks of the campaign were perfect for using the motorcycles as the ground was baked hard in the heat. The bikes could travel quickly and effectively over long distances and often kept pace with the fast moving panzer spearheads. This made operations very effective for delivering dispatches and even hot meals to units that had outstripped their supply columns.

From the beginning of the invasion of Poland and then the Low Countries and France the German war machine quickly paralysed large sections of the enemy railway network, disrupting supplies, knocking out the air force, and outflanking troop operations using Blitzkrieg tactics. In many areas the virtual collapse of the communication system had left commands isolated, making it difficult for them to establish contact with the fronts. Consequently decisions were almost invariably late and therefore disastrously overtaken by events, with the result that one position after another was lost to German hands. Their enemies were faced with the finest fighting army that the world had ever seen. The quality of German weapons – above all the panzers – was of immense importance. Their tactics were the best: stubborn defence, concentrated local firepower from machine guns and mortars, rapid counter-attacks to recover lost ground. Units often fought on even when cut off –

not a mark of fanaticism, but of masterly tactical discipline. The invasion was a product of dazzling organization and staff work and technical ingenuity.

The *Kradschützen Truppen* operated well in the panzer divisions and was able to offer good support and even commit some of its battalions to surprise actions against the enemy. Despite their relatively light armament, with soldiers being armed with the basic equipment of an infantryman with the Karbiner 98K bolt action rifle, many of the rifle squads were equipped with an MG34, which was mounted on the sidecar combination. The majority of motorcycles that saw action between 1939 and 1940 were from the manufacturers BMW or Zündapp. Along the front lines many of these bikes were deployed for immediate action, only the passengers were dismounting and taking up arms against the enemy whilst the motorcycle rider either held back or moved forward using its sidecar combination MG34 as support. In a number of instances the sidecars, which allowed them to carry additional soldiers, were able to provide mobile firepower and could quickly reinforce positions or launch assaults of their own.

On the battlefield motorcycles provided the German Army with increased mobility, allowing for rapid movement of troops and supplies. This was especially valuable for reconnaissance units and swift deployment of infantry and reconnaissance units and formations to various parts of the front lines. These machines were versatile and could operate well on a variety of terrains, including open fields, dirt tracks, and roads, as well as being well-suited to scouting and reconnaissance missions. Their sheer speed allowed reconnaissance units to quickly obtain importation information about enemy positions, strength, and movements. Almost always the motorcycle scouting squads were able to relay the information back to command headquarters rapidly and successfully without hindering operations.

During enemy contact the motorcyclists were able to offer 'hit-and-run' tactics, allowing either armoured troops or infantry to attack vulnerable enemy positions and then withdraw quickly before the enemy could mount a decisive counter-attack. This type of manoeuvre was particularly effective during the early part of the war, when the German forces employed their Blitzkrieg tactics.

Hundreds of motorcycles were used on the battlefield and because they were found to be such a cost-effective option compared to panzers and other motorized vehicles, it made them an attractive choice for many of the army's operational needs and requirements. The machines had characterized the early stages of the war, where speed and manoeuverability were critical and had also proved invaluable in reconnaissance. Every German division had a reconnaissance battalion, usually consisting of a light and heavy armoured car battalion, a motorized infantry battalion, and at least one or more motorcycle companies as well as a number of logistical support companies. All this culminated in the successful conduct of operations. Speed, versatility, and combat effectiveness were key to the motorcycle in the early war years.

(**Above**) Motorcyclists advance along a dusty road during operations in Poland. Motorcyclists could be found in every unit of an infantry and panzer division, especially during the early part of the war. They were even incorporated in the divisional staffs, which included a motorcycle messenger platoon.

(**Opposite, above**) A photograph taken during operations in Poland in September 1939 showing a Wehrmacht patrol unit that has entered a village. A number of local inhabitants appear to have been killed and are lying on the road near a stationary motorcycle combination.

(**Opposite, below**) Out in a field a motorcycle combination can be seen. The rider, and the passenger inside the combination holding a dog, are both wearing the now familiar waterproof coat. All motorcycle units and individual motorcyclists, regardless of rank, were issued with the loose-fitting, rubberized coat. The tails of the coat could be gathered in around the wearer's legs and buttoned in position to allow easier movement while riding the motorcycle.

A *Kradschützen* battalion with motorcycle combination survey a blown bridge over the San River in Poland in September 1939.

A *Kradschützen* battalion can be seen inside a destroyed captured Polish town. During operations through Poland the motorcycle troops were used as couriers or for scouting, and were also part of teams of tank hunters. They supported the divisions of rifle troops and were escorts for the military police. The bikes had other uses that included patrolling, intelligence gathering, including messaging.

A number of Waffen-SS motorcyclists belonging to the 1st Leibstandarte Adolf Hitler Division can be seen advancing through a French town during the German invasion of France in late May 1940. *(NARA)*

Motorcyclists belonging to the 1st Leibstandarte Adolf Hitler Division can be seen on a dusty road during operations in France in June 1940. *(NARA)*

A Waffen-SS motorcyclist wearing the familiar waterproof coat can be seen comically taking a snap of the photographer taking the main photo. *(NARA)*

During the invasion of France an officer can be seen taking a peek at a newspaper being read by a motorcyclist wearing his waterproof coat. Passing by on the road is a motorcycle combination. Note the spare wheel attached to the rear of the combination.

(**Above**) A motorcycle combination can be seen advancing along a congested French road. Much of the German Army in 1940 was still using draught animals to pull the majority of its supplies to the front. Note the pontoon bridge sections also being hauled along the road.

(**Opposite, above**) Wehrmacht infantrymen can be seen marching through a destroyed French town. At the side of the road a motorcyclist dismounts from his BMW R75. Note all the supplies and provisions strapped to the rear of the bike.

(**Opposite, below**) Two stationary motorcycle combinations can be seen at the side of a river inside a captured town. Note the medical cross painted on the sidecar indicating this vehicle was attached to a medical unit.

WH-102722

(**Above**) A motorcyclist converses with an infantryman inside a captured French town in June 1940.

(**Opposite, above**) A motorcycle combination can be seen advancing through a destroyed French town in June 1940. This machine was part of the 3rd Motorcycle Rifle Battalion. The battalion took part in the Western campaign where it advanced to the Albert Canal and was embroiled in the fighting for positions around Dyle.

(**Opposite, below**) A Wehrmacht motorcyclist can be seen stationary on a road during his unit's advance through France in June 1940.

(**Above**) A motorcyclist rides along a road in Holland in May 1940. The motorcycles were versatile, fast, and able to go places more easily than other means of transport like trucks, armoured fighting vehicles, horses and wagons.

(**Opposite, above**) A stationary armoured unit with a motorcycle combination, somewhere in France during operations in June 1940.

(**Opposite, below**) Spread out in the field in order to minimize collateral damage a German unit can be seen. Note the well camouflaged motorcycle combination and the infantryman relaxing inside the sidecar.

In France and a Wehrmacht soldier poses for the camera while eating cheese on the rear of his sidecar combination. Note the well positioned bottle of champagne.

An excellent photograph showing *Kradschützen* Battalion 7 in France in June 1940. The battalion was subordinate to the 7th Panzer Division and took part in the advance through Belgium and northern France to the English Channel.

Two stationary sidecar combinations can be seen in a destroyed French town.

(**Above**) An interesting photograph showing a German unit moving along a road towards the front with a number of motorcycles and motorcycle combinations. Trudging along the side of the road in the opposite direction are French POWs being escorted to the rear.

(**Opposite, above**) A motorcycle combination unit rests inside a captured French town in June 1940. Motorcycle units were basically standard *Schützen* platoons with a little less kit riding on motor bikes and with a platoon car such as a Kfz.13 car or light truck to carry supplies and light mortar.

(**Opposite, below**) A motorcycle combination advances along a dusty road with its unit. Note all the supplies being carried on the combination. Every German division had a motorcycle battalion. It usually consisted of a light and heavy armoured car battalion, a motorized infantry battalion, at least one or more motorcycle companies as well as several logistical support companies. The primary purpose of the motorcycle troops was transmitting orders although this declined as the number and quality of field radios improved.

J-Staffel

NANIA
SUZE

(**Opposite, above**) A column of stationary German vehicles on a main road in France. A motorcycle combination can be seen with the unit. The motorcycles that were attached to motorized infantry units provided mobile fire-power and could quickly reinforce positions or launch assaults.

(**Opposite, below**) Inside a French town and a column of German vehicles including a motorcyclist are advancing along a main road. Moving in the opposite direction are civilian vehicles laden with their possessions.

(**Above**) A motorcycle rider can be seen moving through a destroyed French town. An infantryman hitches a lift on the back of the bike.

A well camouflaged Waffen-SS sidecar combination attached to a *Leibstandarte Kradschützen* Battalion.

Chapter Three

Eastern Front 1941–1943

Between 1940 and 1941 the panzer divisions saw a dramatic expansion, their numbers doubling from ten divisions to twenty. At the same time the *Schützen* – literally 'shooters' but usually translated as 'marksmen' – became the single largest component in the panzer division. A typical *Schützen* brigade was comprised of two *Schützen* regiments (each of two battalions) and a separate *Kradschützen* battalion. In February 1941 the *Schützen* brigade's *Kradschützen* battalion comprised a battalion headquarters of three motorcycle rifle companies, one motorcycle MG company, and one heavy company. Each motorcycle rifle company consisted of eighteen light machine guns, two heavy machine guns, and three 5cm mortars. It also had a machine gun company of eight heavy machine guns and six 8cm mortars.

Surprisingly, even by February 1941 the composition of a standard *Schützen* rifle platoon had not much changed since that of October 1937. A typical *Kradschützen* battalion had three rifle companies and the machine-gun company equipped with motorcycles. In each rifle squad there were twelve men – an NCO, three riflemen, four gunners for two light machine guns and four drivers each with a motorcycle and combination.

During the first months of the war on the Eastern Front the *Kradschützen Truppen* enjoyed much success bucketing across dry open fields and along the hard sun-baked roads. The motorcycles were versatile and fast, and able to go places more readily than other means of transport such as trucks, armoured fighting vehicles, horses and wagons. As in operations against Poland, the Western Front and the Balkans, the *Kradschützen Truppen* continued to be used in Russia for courier dispatches, scouting operations, transporting and escorting officers, carrying riflemen, and hunting and destroying enemy armoured vehicles. Even as the weather changed and heavy rain turned old roadways into a quagmire, the bikes could cope better with the boggy surfaces than any other vehicle.

However, when the snow and freezing winter arrived, even the *Kradschützen* battalions stood motionless along the front lines. Although there had been considerable success during the summer months motorcycle troops had suffered heavy casualties during the campaign, as they did not have the protection or firepower to exist as a separate battalion. The winter of 1941/2 increased the casualty rate and as a consequence a number of *Kradschützen* battalions were disbanded and transferred into the panzer reconnaissance battalions or *Aufklärungsabteilung*. By 1942 these reconnaissance battalions had become highly mobile motorized infantry and panzer divisions equipped with motorcycle combinations such as the BMW R75, Zündapp KS 750, supported by the Volkswagen Kübelwagen and Sd.Kfz.221/222/223 light armoured cars. As with all German combat formations, the composition of the *Aufklärungsabteilung* varied from division to division. Generally though, through 1942 a typical *Aufklärungsabteilungen* attached to a panzer division was equipped with armoured vehicles, with all troops transported in halftracks. These were supported by the *Kradschützen* battalions which were still used in both combat and reconnaissance roles.

Many of the motorcycle battalions were not relegated to reconnaissance operations but continued to fight on the Eastern Front throughout 1942. The German war machine had been badly depleted through the winter of 1941/42 and desperately needed as many fighting units as possible. Even by the beginning of the German summer offensive in May 1942, not all the panzer divisions were fully equipped and ready for combat. Some of the older units, for instance, did not even have their losses from the winter offensive of 1941 replaced and were not fit for any type of full-scale operation. Worn out and depleted panzer divisions were therefore relegated to Army Group North or Army Group Centre, where they were hastily deployed for a series of defensive actions instead. The best-equipped panzer divisions were shifted to Army Group South for operations through the Caucasus, where there were numerous *Kradschützen* battalions to support the spearheads.

By May 1942 most of the panzer divisions involved were up to nearly 85 per cent of their original fighting strength. Various motorcycle rifle battalions continued with varying degrees of success to assist the panzer divisions. Most of these battalions were incorporated into motorized infantry divisions and were regarded as lower-echelon motorized infantry elements which often comprised an infantry regiment (motorized), the infantry battalion (motorized) and the *Kradschützen* battalion (motorcycle rifle battalion). A motorcycle infantry battalion was similar to the motorized infantry battalion and the principal difference, apart from the motorcycles replacing most of the trucks, was the addition of a heavy company with infantry guns, anti-tank guns and an engineer platoon.

Numerous motorcycle rifle battalions were heavily embroiled in fierce fighting throughout 1942. The 3rd Motorcycle Rifle Battalion for instance, fought in the Battle of Kharkov and then advanced into the Caucasus to the Terek. The 4th Motorcycle Rifle Battalion took part in the offensive across the Don and Donets to Stalingrad, but was surrounded and destroyed in the winter of 1942/43. The 6th Motorcycle Rifle

Battalion fought defensive and offensive battles in the Rzhew–Szytschewka–Belyj area from January to April 1942. Following heavy losses it recuperated but was moved to Pochlebin, in the Kalmyk steppe and southwest of Stalingrad, in November 1942. The 16th Motorcycle Rifle Battalion also took part in the German advance across the Don and Donets towards Stalingrad but was destroyed in Stalingrad. The 17th Motorcycle Rifle Battalion was also moved to the Don and took part in the defensive battles around Rostov. The 24th Motorcycle Rifle Battalion fought with the 22nd Panzer Division in the Crimea. In June it was moved southeast of Kharkov and later that year it advanced to the Don for operations against Stalingrad. The 29th Motorcycle Rifle Battalion fought south of Orel. Later in the year the battalion advanced north towards Stalingrad, where it was subsequently destroyed in the Battle of Stalingrad. The 34th Motorcycle Rifle Battalion was deployed in 1942 in the Orel and Bryansk area and was embroiled in fierce fighting. The 53rd Motorcycle Rifle Battalion fought in the Vjazma area. The 59th Motorcycle Rifle Battalion fought towards the Don River and saw heavy fighting in the Rzhev area. The 61st Motorcycle Rifle Battalion took part in the German offensive against the Don and Donets and saw heavy fighting around Stalingrad pocket. The 64th Motorcycle Rifle Battalion saw heavy fighting in southern Russia supporting the main spearheads towards the Don. The 160th Motorcycle Rifle Battalion was yet another that took part in the German offensive towards Stalingrad but was surrounded and destroyed. All of these battalions were later renamed and merged with various Reconnaissance *Abteilungen*.

Three officers walk along a dusty road passing a motorcycle combination during operations in the Balkans in 1941. The advance through the Balkans was often perilous, especially for wheeled vehicles, which frequently became stuck along muddy roads. (*NARA*)

(**Above**) A Luftwaffe motorcyclist can be seen on the road. The machine appears to be a 1941 model of the NSU 251 OLS Motorcycle used extensively by the Wehrmacht and the Luftwaffe. It had a 10bhp 1 cylinder 4 stroke engine with a top speed of 62.5mph.

(**Opposite, above**) Taken during the opening phase of Operation Barbarossa, the German invasion of the Soviet Union, and a column of German vehicles can be seen inside a captured Russian town. A motorcyclist is escorting Russian POWs along the street to the rear.

(**Opposite, below**) *Truppen* from a Waffen-SS *Kradschützen* battalion seen in a field with a Pz.Kpfw.III. *(NARA)*

A combination pictured on a road supporting a column of vehicles during the early part of Operation Barbarossa in the summer of 1941. The passenger, wearing the rubberised motorcycle coat, is sleeping. Note the divisional insignia painted on the front of the sidecar indicating it belongs to the LVI *Armee-Korps* (mot.).

A combination in operation on the Eastern Front in the early autumn of 1941. The bucket attached to the vehicle appears to contain whitewash required to paint vehicles for winter operations. During this early period of the war winter whitewash paint was not universally found in either the Waffen-SS or Wehrmacht divisions.

Two Waffen-SS combinations have halted on a road and the riders tuck into rations before resuming their drive.

Two motorcyclists laden with supplies complete with panniers can be seen advancing along a road past a group of bewildered Russian civilians. *(NARA)*

A Waffen-SS NCO converses with his commanding officer who has hitched a lift on a BMW R75 motorcycle. *(NARA)*

A motorcycle combination and a motorcycle attached to a *Leibstandarte* Waffen-SS *Kradschützen* battalion are escorting Russian POWs along a dusty road. *(NARA)*

A Waffen-SS motorcycle combination passes a Wehrmacht combination escorting Soviet POWs. *(NARA)*

Two motorcycle combinations attached to a *Totenkopf* (Death's Head) Waffen-SS *Kradschützen* battalion cross over a wooden bridge during operations on the Eastern Front in summer 1941. (*NARA*)

Seen here is are *Totenkopf* motorcycle combinations on the road during combat operations in Russia in the summer of 1941. (*NARA*)

Two photographs showing *Totenkopf* combinations on the advance along a road during combat operations in Russia during the summer of 1941. *(NARA)*

Seen here is a motorcycle rider wearing aviator goggles that all German motorcyclists used to protect their eyes from the wind and dust. *(NARA)*

Motorcycle combination riders wearing the familiar aviator goggles. *(NARA)*

A Waffen-SS motorcyclist pays his respects to fallen comrades at the side of the road where they have been buried. *(NARA)*

Staged propaganda image: Waffen-SS troops read their official newspaper, *Das Schwarze Korps* (*The Black Corps*). It was published on Wednesdays and distributed free of charge. All SS members were encouraged to read it. *(NARA)*

Staged propaganda image: Waffen-SS panzer crewmen in their black uniforms reading the Nazi *Völkischer Beobachter* (*The Peoples' Observer*) newspaper. (NARA)

The first of five photographs showing Waffen-SS motorcyclists and combination riders struggling to negotiate some of the typical roads on the Eastern Front in the summer of 1941. Many were no more than dirt tracks and when it rained they quickly turned into quagmires, making it almost impossible for the motorcycles to get along. *(NARA)*

Three photographs taken in sequence, showing a number of Waffen-SS *Totenkopf* motorcyclists escorting a column of light vehicles containing commanding officers during operations on the Eastern Front in summer 1941. *(NARA)*

(**Below**) A stranded Wehrmacht motorcycle rider with his bike that has developed a mechanical issue in a river of mud in Russia, 1941. Although these machines were versatile over many terrains, snow and mud hindered their mobility. In fact, the mud produced from a few hours of rain in Russia was enough to immobilize whole columns of wheeled transport, even tanks.

A motorcycle combination stuck in a muddy quagmire has been abandoned by its rider. Note the sidecar insignia indicating it belongs to the Waffen-SS *Totenkopf* division. (NARA)

The first of two photographs showing the difficulties motorcyclists endured following a heavy downpour of rain on the antiquated Russian road system.

A motorcyclist wearing his familiar summer camouflage Waffen-SS smock and carrying a Karbiner 98K bolt action rifle. Many motorcycles were utilized for reconnaissance in the field. Note the spare wheel attached to the bike. *(NARA)*

A motorcyclist escorts Russian POWs through a village. Note the military policeman, a member of the *Feldgendarmerie* who were employed in occupied areas, in Wehrmacht, Waffen-SS and Luftwaffe military police units with army divisions and higher formations. These soldiers were responsible for policing the military and were given specific duties of arresting deserters, directing military traffic and evacuating and moving refugees, along with transportation of prisoners. (*NARA*)

Two shots of the same motorcyclist in the summer of 1941 in Russia. Motorcyclists could be found in every unit of an infantry and panzer division, especially during the early part of the war. They were even incorporated in the divisional staffs, which included a motorcycle messenger platoon. (*NARA*)

Waffen-SS riders watch an engineer fixing a telephone cable. The motorcycle was used for both combat and reconnaissance roles. Each infantry and panzer division incorporated hundreds of machines among the panzer and rifle regiments, flak detachments, artillery regiments, supply units, signals and reconnaissance. *(NARA)*

A Waffen-SS motorcycle combination bucketing along a muddy road. (*NARA*)

A Waffen-SS *Totenkopf* combination struggles to manoeuvre along a muddy road and rider and passenger dismount from the bike to give a helping hand. Traversing the great expanses of Russia motorcycles were inevitably prone to mechanical faults and as a consequence a well-equipped motorcycle workshop supported the vast number of machines deployed on the Eastern Front, especially in 1941. (*NARA*)

A *Totenkopf* soldier directs a medical sidecar combination towards an injured comrade in a field during a lull in the fighting on the Eastern Front in 1941. *(NARA)*

Two photographs taken in sequence show a Waffen-SS motorcycle combination on a railway line. As with all motorcyclists in both the Wehrmacht and Waffen-SS, there was a kinship among these soldiers who called themselves *Kradmelder* (dispatch riders). However, they rode exposed, often without support of armoured vehicles or infantry beside them. As a consequence they were regarded as moving targets by the enemy and many were killed by snipers, minefields, artillery fire and strafing aircraft. *(NARA)*

Two photographs showing a motorcycle being transported by rail. In the first the machine is being secured to the flatbed railcar and the second shows a BMW R75 being removed from the flatbed. Moving troops and vehicles by rail was important for speed and efficiency in both infantry and panzer divisions during the war. *(NARA)*

The first of four photographs taken in sequence show a Waffen-SS reconnaissance unit surveying the burning wreckage of a Russian vehicle. Although a large number of motorcyclists during the early years of the war rode into battle and dismounted to fight, both motorcycles and motorcyclists were regarded as vulnerable to small-arms fire and booby traps. *(NARA)*

161417

A reconnaissance unit on scouting patrol. Early in the war motorcyclists were used extensively for reconnaissance duties. Their very versatile machines enabled them to survey enemy positions until they encountered enemy fire and then to return swiftly with important information relating to the location and strength of the enemy. *(NARA)*

Photograph taken from within an Sd.Kfz.251 halftrack during what appears to be a reconnaissance mission somewhere on the Eastern Front. The image depicts a motorcycle rider and a combination following two Sd.Kfz.251 halftracks along a road. *(NARA)*

A combination advances past burning buildings during operations in Russia in 1942.

Part of a Waffen-SS *Kradschützen* battalion with their fully loaded combinations during a pause in the unit's advance into Russia. (*NARA*)

The versatility of the combination meant that the machine could also be adapted to retrieve wounded soldiers from the battlefield and stretcher them to the nearest field hospital, as this photo depicts. *(NARA)*

An SS motorcyclist attached to the Waffen-SS *Totenkopf* Division drinks from his canteen during a lull in the advance. *(NARA)*

Part of a *Leibstandarte* Waffen-SS *Kradschützen* battalion are advancing along a road. Attached to the motorcycles are leather saddlebags containing the rider's personal kit and maps or paperwork. Leather and canvas were most commonly used material for the saddlebags and kept the items stored inside relatively protected from the elements. *(NARA)*

Part of a Waffen-SS *Leibstandarte* reconnaissance detachment or the *Aufklärungsabteilung*. Even the Waffen-SS reconnaissance detachments varied from division to division and from one period of the war to another. In the *Leibstandarte* the *Aufklärungsabteilungen* was generally equipped with armoured vehicles, and all troops were transported in halftracks including BMW R75, Zündapp KS 750, Volkswagen Kubelwagens and Sd.KKz.221/222/223 light armoured cars. *(NARA)*

The first of six photographs depicting a *Leibstandarte* Waffen-SS *Kradschützen* battalion attached to a reconnaissance detachment, with their combinations. These detachments often operated in mixed teams gathered from various companies that included the motorcycles and other vehicles. The vehicles had to move quickly on the battlefield but many missions were dangerous and losses among motorcycle teams were high. However, due to losses through 1942 it was decided to start merging the motorcycle and reconnaissance battalions. Most motorcycle battalions retained their designation, whereas only a few of the reconnaissance battalions kept theirs. *(NARA)*

(**Below**) Motorcycles advance along a road during a reconnaissance mission. As early as late 1941, early 1942, there was a slow conversion of both Wehrmacht and Waffen-SS motorcycle-equipped reconnaissance companies to armoured halftracks, or Volkswagens. Initially the companies continued to use the motorcycle designation but they were gradually being equipped with Volkswagens for more and more reconnaissance roles.

Two photographs show motorcyclists resting during a pause in operations on the Eastern Front. Motorcycles served a variety of roles in Russia, contributing to German military mobility, reconnaissance capability, and operational flexibility. They were particularly well-suited to operations where speed and manoeuvrability were critical to success.

Two photos taken in sequence showing two motorcyclists resting and playing cards during a lull in operations. By late 1942 motorcycles were being used less as German infantry and panzer divisions began to go on the defensive. By early 1943 battle groups were considered more effective. These were called *Kampfgruppen* and comprised a combination of tanks, infantry, and artillery (including anti-tank) elements, generally organized to carry out a particular task or operation. As a result motorcycles would no longer be attack vehicles, but used for dispatch purposes instead, without their sidecars.

Wehrmacht infantry at a water well, a motorcycle combination can be seen parked nearby.

Chapter Four

Last Years: Relegation

In the Wehrmacht and Waffen-SS reconnaissance was often a sophisticated and complex undertaking, and the reconnaissance battalion was a key component of all divisions. This was especially so for the mechanized mobile divisions and their reconnaissance battalions. The tactical doctrine of the employment of the reconnaissance battalion was that it should fight for information. Locating the enemy was regarded as only the initial stage of a recon operation. The reconnaissance battalion was then expected to develop the situation by forcing the enemy to deploy, and subsequently reveal his strength and intention. This was undertaken by simulating a full-scale attack, both to acquire and report vital information. For a successful reconnaissance operation a recon battalion had to have sufficient strength and firepower for the attack and reliable means of communication with the divisional headquarters.

In 1941 a typical reconnaissance battalion of a panzer division was comprised of a motorized reconnaissance battalion of one armoured car squadron, one motorcycle infantry Ccmpany and one heavy company for both panzer and motorized infantry divisions. By 1943 armoured reconnaissance varied in size and structure. A typical battalion often comprised of a halftrack armoured car squadron. However, this was often replaced by motorcycle or light motorized companies with Volkswagen cars.

During 1943, when the tide of war turned against the German war machine on the Eastern Front, the Germans were forced to develop defensive strategies as they were slowly pushed back by the ever increasing strength and resources of Russian and Anglo-American forces. As a result of the growing pressure, apart from the more powerful reconnaissance battalions the Germans developed the *Kampfgruppe* or battle group as an ad hoc combined arms formation. On the battlefield they were usually employed in a combination of tanks, infantry, artillery, and anti-tank elements for a particular task or operation.

A *Kampfgruppe* could range in size from a company to a corps. For this reason and because of the urgent requirement to sustain the Germans on the battlefield, large formations of lightly armed *Kradschützen* motorcycle troops were made obsolete in the first half of 1943, the soldiers being transferred to other services such as panzer grenadier regiments, *Kampfgruppen* and reconnaissance *Abteilung*-sized formations. Those motorcycle troops that were not absorbed into the *Kampfgruppen* for the remainder of the war were relegated to support roles such as despatch riders, messengers and light reconnaissance duties. These motorcyclists were to perform their duties as special motorized, infantry-based reconnaissance units with the sole objective of quickly penetrating enemy lines and locating and/or harassing any enemy forces primarily to determine their size, strength and location. The motorcyclists were often supported by halftracks. However, by 1943 motorcycle companies had double the number of light machine guns that would have been found in a 1941 company. There were also troops now equipped in the same way but mounted on *Kettenkrads*.

The *Kettenkrad* was a halftrack motorcycle with a single wheel. Technically the *Kettenkrad* had started its life as a light tractor for airborne troops. However, on the Eastern Front it proved to be reliable, robust and well suited to bad roads, thick mud and snow. They were highly versatile machines and were used by *Wehrmacht*, *Waffen-SS*, *Luftwaffe*, and motorcycle troops for scouting, fast infantry transports, cable laying and a variety of other tasks.

Throughout 1944 the *Kettenkrads* became a common feature on the battlefield within all elements of the panzer divisions. The panzer divisions themselves by this late period of the war were using a streamlined version of the organization which included a single panzer regiment with two battalions, two panzer grenadier regiments, each with two battalions, an artillery regiment with one self-propelled and two towed battalions, an armoured reconnaissance battalion including *Kradschützen Truppen*, an antitank battalion, a flak battalion, a pioneer (combat engineer) battalion; plus the usual divisional service units. By the latter part of 1944 the reconnaissance battalion had become a very powerful unit equipped with a mix of wheeled and halftrack armoured cars. Generally the whole battalion was supposed to be equipped with armoured halftracks, but often it was compelled to supply one or two of the reconnaissance companies with the Volkswagen light field car instead, complete with motorcycle combinations.

As the Eastern and Western Fronts receded, losses among what was left of the reconnaissance battalions mounted. This included the motorcycle riders. Many motorcycles either could not be refuelled or were lost in action, leaving the soldiers to be absorbed into various *Kampfgruppen* and taking up defensive action.

In spite its demise on the battlefield and its relegation to generally light reconnaissance roles in the latter part of the war, nothing could take away from the fact that the German military had perfected the use of the motorcycle on the battlefield. It had shown its worth as a rapid mobile assault and reconnaissance force which had become an integral part in the German Blitzkrieg successes of 1939–40. Although they became more or less obsolete for this purpose by the mid-war period and were transferred to other services such as panzer grenadier regiments and *Kampfgruppen*, the motorcycle still proved its worth in a number of supporting roles for the remainder of the war.

The first of three photographs taken in sequence, showing a motorcyclist caked in mud due to negotiating the muddy Russian roads after a downpour of rain.

During operations in Italy in 1943 two photographs taken in sequence show a motorcyclist from a Waffen-SS *Leisbstandarte KradSchützen* battalion painting an SS licence plate on an R75 BMW combination. (*NARA*)

A motorcycle dispatch rider halted on the road consults a map. By 1943 the German army had become increasingly dependent on motorcycle units for reconnaissance duties. *(NARA)*

A Waffen-SS motorcyclist wearing the winter reversible grey side out, driving along a muddy road during winter operations in early 1943.

Winter-clad combination riders stationary on the side of a road while a whitewashed Tiger tank passes, during winter operations on the Eastern Front. By 1943 the *Kradschützen* battalions were slowly incorporated into various panzer reconnaissance *Abteilungen*.

Two photographs showing a reconnaissance *Abteilung* on a road somewhere on the Eastern Front in 1943.

Waffen-SS *Kradschützen* battalion supporting an armoured column of Sd.Kfz.251 halftracks during a reconnaissance mission. (*NARA*)

The first of ten photographs show the Sd.Kfz.2 halftrack motorcycle in a variety of roles on the Eastern Front between 1941 and 1944. Although not technically a motorcycle the vehicle was in effect a halftrack motorcycle with a single wheel, known as the Kleines Kettenkraftrad HK 101. Initially it was used as a light tractor for airborne troops. Later soldiers used these vehicles extensively on the Eastern Front for laying communication cables and moving supplies from one part of the front to another. In the latter part of the war there were reconnaissance *Abteilung*-sized formations with motorcycles which carried out various recon duties including carrying troops into battle.

(**Below**) A motorcycle combination, part of a reconnaissance *Abteilung* on the Eastern Front. *(NARA)*

A motorcycle combination can be seen supporting a Panther and Sd.Kf.251 halftrack on the Eastern Front. As a means to sustain the German army on the battlefield large formations of lightly armed *Kradschützen* motorcycle troops were made obsolete in the first half of 1943. The soldiers were transferred to other services such as panzer grenadier regiments, *Kampfgruppen* and reconnaissance *Abteilung*-sized formations.

A combination halted in a field, supporting a number of Sd.Kfz.251 halftrack personnel carriers during a reconnaissance mission. (*NARA*)

Waffen-SS panzer reconnaissance *Abteilung* advancing along a road in combinations. Due to shortages in the field there were numerous variations from a standard reconnaissance *Abteilung*. Some battalions had only one armoured reconnaissance company, sometimes supplemented by a motorcycle infantry company or a light motorized company with Volkswagen field cars. *(NARA)*

A Waffen-SS combination moving through a Russian village. Note the MG34 machine gun attached to the sidecar. *(NARA)*

The first of four photographs depicting the 7th SS Volunteer Mountain Division 'Prinz Eugen' during operations in Yugoslavia. These soldiers are part of the 7th SS Motorcycle Rifle Battalion. *(NARA)*

A photograph showing dismounted infantry from the 11th SS motorcycle Regiment of the 11th SS Volunteer Panzergrenadier Division Nordland during operations in Croatia. *(NARA)*

(**Above**) A Waffen-SS motorcyclist making minor mechanical adjustments to his BMW motorcycle during operations on the Eastern Front in 1943. *(NARA)*

(**Opposite**) A motorcycle combination during a reconnaissance mission in the Balkans in 1944. *(NARA)*

(**Below**) *Leibstandarte* panzer reconnaissance *Abteilung* advances through an Italian town during operations in 1944. These vehicles are attached to the 1st SS Panzer Reconnaissance Battalion. *(NARA)*

A sidecar combination can be seen flanking a column of Pz.Kpfw.IV tanks through Rome in 1944. These vehicles belong to the 1st SS *Leibstandarte* Panzer Division. *(NARA)*

Fallschirmjager (paratrooper) motorcycle troops scrutinizing a map during operations in northern France in 1944.

Fallschirmjager motorcycle combination with MG34 halted on a road in late 1944 on the Western Front.

Appendix I

Components of a *Kradschützen* Battalion

1937–39

KStN 1109 Headquarters, Motorcycle Infantry Battalion

Battalion Headquarters: 5 motorcycles, 1 car
Signal Detachment, Headquarters Section: 1 car
2 Pack Radio Sections: 1 car
12 Light Armoured Radio Section: 1 radio armoured car
Maintenance Detachment: 1 motorcycle, 1 car (light), 2 trucks (light), 2 trucks (2-ton)
Trains: 3 motorcycles, 2 cars (light), 3 trucks (light), 1 truck (2-ton), 1 ambulance

KStN 1111 Motorcycle Infantry Company

Company Heaquarters: 3 motorcycles
1 Motorcycle: 1 car, 1 car
3 Motorcycle Platoon, Headquarters Section: 2 motorcycles, 1 car, 1 car
3 Motorcycle Squadron: 3 motorcycles, 1 Infantry Squad with 1 light machine gun
1 Mortar Sections: 2 motorcycles, 1 mortar (50mm)
Machine Gun Detachment: 10 motorcycles, 2 heavy machine guns
Company Trains: 2 motorcycles, 1 car, 1 truck (light), 5 trucks (1.5-ton)

KStN 1118 Motorcycle Machine Gun Company

Headquarters: 3 motorcycles
1 motorcycle, 1 car, 1 truck
2 Light Tele Section: 1 car
2 Machine Gun Platoons, Headquarters Section: 1 motorcycle, 1 car, 1 car
1 Light Tele Section: 1 car
Ammunition Section: 2 motorcycles
2 Heavy Machine Gun Squadron: 6 motorcycles, 2 heavy machine guns
1 Mortar Platoon, Headquarters Section: 1 motorcycle, 1car, 1 truck
3 Mortar Section: 1 car, 2 trucks, 2 mortars (81mm)
Company Trains: 2 motorcycles, 1 car, 1 truck (light), 5 trucks (2-ton)

KStN 1121 Motorized Heavy Company

Company Headquarters: 2 motorcycles, 1 car

Company Trains: 3 motorcycles, 1 car (medium); 5 trucks (2-ton); 1 truck (medium)

KStN 1122 Platoon

Headquarters Section: 2 motorcyles, 1 truck

Gun Section: 4 trucks, 3 ATG (37mm – towed); 1 light machine gun

KStN 1123 Light Platoon

Headquarters Section: 3 motorcycles, 1 car

1 Light Tele Section: 1 car

Gun Section: 1 motorcycle; 3 trucks, 2 light IG artillery (75mm – towed), 1 trailer (ammo)

KStN 1124 Engineer Platoon

Headquarters Section: 4 motorcycles, 3 cars

Engineering Section: 2 trucks (3-ton), 1 Engineer Section, 1 Light Machine Gun

1940

Headquarters, Motorized Infantry Battalion

Battalion Headquarters: 8 motorcycles, 1 car, 1 car

Signal Detachment, Headquarters Section: 1 car

2 Light Tele Section: 1 car

2 Pack Radio Section: 1 car

2 Light Armoured Radio Section: 1 radio armoured car

Battalion Maintenance Detachment: 1 motorcycle, 1 car (light), 2 trucks (light); 2 trucks (2-ton)

Battalion Trains: 3 motorcycles, 2 cars (light), 3 trucks (light), 1 truck (2-ton), 1 ambulance

Light Motorized Transport Column, Motorized Infantry Regiment

Headquarters Section: 2 motorcycles, 1 car (medium)

Transport Platoon: 1 motorcycle, 13 trucks (light)

Trains: 1 car (light), 3 trucks (light).

Motorcycle Infantry Company

Company Headquarters: 4 motorcycles, 1 car, 1 car

3 Motorcycles Platoon, Headquarters Section: 2 motorcycles, 2 cars

3 Motorcycles Squadron: 4 motorcycles, 1 Infantry Squad, 2 light machine guns

1 Mortar Section: 1 truck, 1 mortar (50mm)

1 Motorcycle Machine Gun Platoon, Headquarters Section: 3 motorcycles, 1 car, 1 car

1 Light Tele Section: 1 car

2 Heavy Machine Gun Section: 7 motorcycles, 2 heavy machine guns

Company Trains: 2 motorcycles, 1 car, 1 truck (light), 5 trucks (2-ton)

KStN 1121 Motorized Heavy Company
Company Headquarters: 4 motorcycles, 1 car
Trains: 3 motorcycles, 1 car (medium), 5 trucks (2-ton), 1 truck (medium)
KStN 1122 ATG Platoon
Headquarters Section: 2 motorcycles, 1 truck
Gun Section: 4 trucks, 3 ATG (37mm – towed), 1 light machine gun
KStN 1123 IG Platoon
Headquarters Section: 3 motorcycles, 1 car
Light Tele Section: 1 car
Gun Section: 1 motorcycle, 3 trucks, 2 light IG (75mm – towed), 1 trailer (ammo)
KStN 1126 Mortar Platoon
Headquarters Section: 1 motorcycle, 1 car
Mortar Section: 3 trucks, 2 mortars (81mm)

Appendix II

Motorcycle Rifle Battalions 1939–43

Kradschützen or motorcycle troops were a common part of German panzer divisions until late 1942, by which time they had largely been replaced by panzer grenadiers mounted in armoured carriers. Their manpower was often recruited from former cavalry units or reorganized machine-gun battalions.

1st Motorcycle Rifle Battalion

The *Kradschützen* Battalion 1 was formed on 15 October 1935 in Bad Freienwalde (Oder). The battalion and was subordinate to the 1st Panzer Division. The battalion took part in the Polish and western campaigns. From June 1941 the battalion fought in Russia. On 1 June 1942, it was reorganized and included the Panzer Reconnaissance 4.

2nd Motorcycle Rifle Battalion

The *Kradschützen* Battalion 2 was formed on 15 October 1935 in Bad Freienwalde (Oder). The battalion was subordinate to the 2nd Panzer Division and was stationed in Eisenach. On 12 October 1937, the battalion moved to Bad Kissingen, in Military District XIII. The battalion was later stationed in Eisenstadt, Wehrkreis XVII. In 1938 the battalion took part in the invasion of the Sudetenland and in 1939 in the invasion of the remainder of Czechoslovakia. Also in 1939 the battalion took part in the Polish campaign and then in 1940 in the western campaign and the campaign against Greece. From June 1941, it took part in operations against Russia. On 16 March 1942, the 1st company of the Panzer Reconnaissance *Abteilung* 5 was taken over as the 1st Panzer Reconnaissance Company.

3rd Motorcycle Rifle Battalion

The *Kradschützen* Battalion 3 was formed on 15 October 1935 in Bad Freienwalde (Oder). The battalion was subordinate to the 3rd Panzer Division. The Breslau State Police Motorcycle Rifle unit provided the core for the 3rd company. At the beginning of the Polish campaign, the battalion took part in operations in Poland and fought with the 3rd Panzer Division in the Tuchel area. It then moved and fought in areas in Bielsk and Brest-Litovsk. It then moved south of Wlodawa. When operations were completed in Poland the battalion moved back to its home garrisons, where it remained until the end of October 1939. From the beginning of November 1939, the battalion moved with the 3rd Panzer Division to the Western Front. From 10 May 1940 it took part in the Western campaign where it advanced to the Albert Canal and was embroiled in the fighting for positions around Dyle. After the Battle of Flanders, the battalion took part in the fighting on the Somme in early June. On 12 June the battalion crossed the Marne towards Dijon and Beaune. After the end of the Western campaign, the battalion returned to its home base.

At the end of May 1941, the battalion left its peacetime base for the last time and moved to the Brest-Litovsk area. From 22 June 1941, the battalion fought on the Eastern Front. It took part in operations around Bialystok and Minsk, crossed the Beressina near Bobruisk and the Dnieper. After the Battle of Kiev the battalion took part in fighting around Vjazma and Bryansk and advanced towards Orel. This was followed by the offensive battles from Moscow to Tula and the subsequent defensive battles. In February 1942, the battalion fought in the Kursk area on the upper Donets. On 25 April 1942, the battalion was merged with the 1st Panzer Reconnaissance. It fought in the Battle of Kharkov and then advanced into the Caucasus to the Terek. At the beginning of January 1943, it withdrew from the Caucasus to the Don. From the beginning of March 1943 the battalion fought in the Donets region and until the beginning of March 1943 between the Donets and the Dnieper. It then undertook defensive fighting in areas around Mius. On 28 April 1943, the battalion was renamed Panzer Reconnaissance *Abteilung* 3.

4th Motorcycle Rifle Battalion

The *Kradschützen* Battalion 4 was established on 1 December 1941 at the Stablack military training area, in Military District I. The battalion was created through the reorganization of the Cycling *Abteilung* 1. It was subordinate to the 24th Panzer Division. Following training the battalion moved to Russia in the Kursk area at the end of May 1942 and from here took part in the offensive across the Don and Donets to Stalingrad in the summer of 1942, where it was surrounded and destroyed in the winter of 1942/3. On 17 February 1943 the battalion was reorganized in France as Panzer Reconnaissance *Abteilung* 4.

6th Motorcycle Rifle Battalion

The *Kradschützen* Battalion 6 was formed on 1 April 1939 from the IV Squadron of Cavalry Rifle Regiment 4 at Iserlohn Military District VI for the 1st Light Division. The battalion took part in the Polish campaign. On 18 October the 1st Light Division was reorganized into the 6th Panzer Division. On 10 May 1940, the 6th Panzer Division crossed the Belgian border with *Kradschützen* Battalion 6 and advanced through the Ardennes. On 13/14 May it crossed over the Meuse at Montherme and the battalion advanced to the Oise. The battalion took part in the battles for Flanders and on

27 May fought for Cassel, Hazebrouk and Poperinghe. After the Battle of Northern France, the battalion prepared for the 'Battle of France'. Following the successful battle for France on 1 July 1940 the battalion moved back to its peacetime location.

On 1 August 1940 the 3rd Motorcycle Rifle Squadron was handed over to Motorcycle Rifle Battalion 16 of the 16th Panzer Division. This squadron was replaced by the 2nd company of the 79th Infantry Regiment. In June 1941 the battalion took part in the campaign against Russia. From October 1941, the battalion attacked eastwards across the upper Dnieper towards Moscow. The battalion played a key role in the crossing over the Volga near Kalinin. The battalion then attacked via Klin-Rogachev to the Moskva–Volga Canal northeast of Nikolskoye. From January to April 1942, defensive and offensive battles were fought in the Rzhew–Szytschewka–Belyj area.

In April 1942 the battalion was moved to France for recuperation and additional training. It returned to the southern sector of the Eastern Front in November 1942 and fought near Pochlebin, in the Kalmyk steppe and southwest of Stalingrad. It took part in the German relief efforts on Stalingrad. Following its failed relief efforts the battalion moved to the Bogutchar area in order to prevent a Russian breakthrough. On 1 February 1943, the battalion was incorporated into Panzer Reconnaissance *Abteilung* 57 and formed the Panzer Reconnaissance *Abteilung* 6 on 1 April 1943.

7th Motorcycle Rifle Battalion

The *Kradschützen* Battalion 7 was formed on 25 October 1939 from the 1st Battalion of the disbanded Reconnaissance Regiment 7 at the peacetime base in Bad Kissingen in Military District IX. The battalion was subordinate to the 7th Panzer Division. At the end of 1939 the battalion moved with the 7th Panzer Division to the Bonn–Bad Neuenahr area to prepare for the Western campaign. In May 1940 the battalion took part in the advance through Belgium and northern France to the English Channel. It fought against the British breakout attacks at Arras. During the second phase of the Western campaign, the battalion advanced through the Weygand Line to Rouen from 5 June 1940 and then marched across the Seine to Le Havre–Cherbourg and via Rennes to the Charente. After the Western campaign, the battalion remained in France and returned to its home base in January 1941. The battalion was brought to full strength and received its third motorbike company. In June 1941 the battalion moved to East Prussia and took part in the war against Russia. In the spring of 1942, the remnants of Panzer Reconnaissance *Abteilung* 37 were incorporated into the battalion to strengthen it. On 1 April 1943, it was renamed as Panzer Reconnaissance *Abteilung* 7.

8th Motorcycle Rifle Battalion

The *Kradschützen* Battalion 8 was formed on 1 April 1940 from the 2nd *Abteilung* of the 9th Cavalry Rifle Regiment at the Sorau Military District III. The battalion was subordinated to the 8th Panzer Division and took part in the Western campaign in

1940. In the spring of 1941 it was sent to the Balkans and from June 1941 to the Eastern Front. On 25 January 1942 remnants of Panzer Reconnaissance *Abteilung* 59 was incorporated into the battalion. On 1 April 1 1943, it was renamed as Panzer Reconnaissance *Abteilung* 8.

10th Motorcycle Rifle Battalion

The *Kradschützen* Battalion 10 was created on 1 March 1941 from elements of Rifle Regiment 69 and the Rifle Regiment 86. The battalion's peacetime location was Sorau in Military District III. The battalion was subordinated to the 10th Panzer Division where it fought in Russia from June 1941. In May 1942, the battalion moved with the division to France and prepared for a deployment to North Africa. In November 1942 the battalion moved to North Africa. On March 24, 1943 the battalion was renamed Panzer Reconnaissance *Abteilung* 10.

13th Motorcycle Rifle Battalion

The *Kradschützen* Battalion 13 was formed on 6 August 1942 through the reorganization of Reconnaissance *Abteilung* 22. On 5 September 1942, a tank scout company 13 was added. The battalion was subordinated to the 22nd Infantry Division where it was sent to Greece. On 2 October 1942, the battalion was renamed Reconnaissance *Abteilung* 22.

15th Motorcycle Rifle Battalion

The *Kradschützen* Battalion 15 was formed on 11 November 1940 in Military District XII. The battalion's peacetime location was Salzwedel in Military District XI. The battalion was subordinated to the 15th Panzer Division. The battalion moved to North Africa in the spring of 1941 and took part in operations with the *Afrika Korps*. By late 1942 the battalion was reorganized as III Battalion of the 104th Rifle Regiment of the 21st Panzer Division.

16th Motorcycle Rifle Battalion

The *Kradschützen* Battalion 16 was established on 2 August 1940 in Bielefeld, in Military District VI, by reorganizing the Machine Gun Battalion 1. The battalion was subordinated to the 16th Panzer Division. The battalion was a training unit in Romania from December 1940 and took part in the Balkan campaign in April 1941. From June 1941 the battalion fought in Russia. On 1 August 1941, it merged with Panzer Reconnaissance *Abteilung* 16. In 1942 the battalion took part in the German advance across the Don and Donets towards Stalingrad. In January 1943 the battalion was destroyed in Stalingrad. On 1 April 1943, the battalion was renamed Panzer Reconnaissance *Abteilung* 16.

17th Motorcycle Rifle Battalion

The *Kradschützen* Battalion 17 was established on 11 October 1940 in Military District VII through the reorganization of the 2nd Battalion of the 63rd Infantry

Regiment. The battalion's peacetime location was Ingolstadt. The battalion was subordinated to the 17th Panzer Division where it was moved with the battalion and fought on the Eastern Front. It took part in the battles for Smolensk, Kiev and Bryansk in central Russia and at the end of 1941 fought on the Moscow Front in the Tula area. On 1 April 1942, Panzer Reconnaissance *Abteilung* 27 was incorporated into the battalion and was deployed in the Orel area. At the end of the year it moved to the Don and took part in the defensive battles around Rostov. On 1 May 1943 it was renamed Panzer-Einklarungs-*Abteilung* 17.

18th Motorcycle Rifle Battalion

The *Kradschützen* Battalion 18 was created on 15 October 1940 in Military District IV, from the motorized 1st Battalion, 52nd Infantry Regiment. The battalion was subordinated to the 18th Panzer Division. It was sent to the Eastern Front in June 1941 and by November it was incorporated into the reinforced by Panzer Reconnaissance *Abteilung* 88. On 1 April 1943, the *Abteilung* was renamed Panzer Reconnaissance *Abteilung* 18. By October 1943 the battalion was absorbed into Rifle Division 88.

19th Motorcycle Rifle Battalion

The *Kradschützen* Battalion 19 was formed on 1 November 1940 in Military District XI, through the reorganization of the 1st Battalion of the 73rd Infantry Regiment. The battalion's peacetime location was Celle. The battalion was subordinated to the 19th Panzer Division where it fought in Russia from June 1941. On 14 August 1941 the battalion was disbanded and the remnants were incorporated into Panzer Reconnaissance *Abteilung* 19.

20th Motorcycle Rifle Battalion

The *Kradschützen* Battalion 20 was created on 4 November 1940 in Bielefeld, in Military District VI, through the reorganization of the III. The battalion's peacetime location was Worms. The battalion was subordinated to the 20th Panzer Division and fought on the Eastern Front from June 1941. In 1942 Panzer Reconnaissance *Abteilung* 92 was incorporated. On 1 April 1943, the battalion was renamed Panzer Reconnaissance *Abteilung* 20.

22nd Motorcycle Rifle Battalion

The *Kradschützen* Battalion 22 was established up in Greifswald on 20 August 1940 by *Wehrkreis* (military district) II. The battalion was subordinated to the 2nd Infantry Division (motorized), and from 5 October 1940 to the 12th Panzer Division. The battalion was sent to the Eastern Front in June 1941and suffered heavy losses during its first few months in the Leningrad area. In 1942 following recuperation the battalion moved to the German central area around Jarzewo. Once again over a period of months the battalion suffered heavy losses. On 20 April 1943, the battalion was renamed Panzer Reconnaissance *Abteilung* 12.

23rd Motorcycle Rifle Battalion

The *Kradschützen* Battalion 23 was formed on 13 September 1941 in France. The battalion was subordinated to the 23rd Panzer Division. From March 1942 the battalion fought in Russia. On 22 April 1943, the battalion was renamed Panzer Reconnaissance *Abteilung* 23. It then merged with the remnants of *Kradschützen* Battalion 24 of the 22nd Panzer Division.

24th Motorcycle Rifle Battalion

The *Kradschützen* Battalion 24 was created on 10 September 1941 in France. The battalion was subordinated to the 22nd Panzer Division and was deployed in the Niort area in southwest France. On 17 February 1942 the battalion was transferred to the Eastern Front with the 22nd Panzer Division where it fought in the Crimea. In June it was moved southeast of Kharkov. Later that year it advanced to the Don for operations against Stalingrad. In mid-September the battalion moved to the area around Millerowo, where the 22nd Panzer Division was assembled. By February 1943 the battalion was removed from its positions on the Donets and fought in the Sverdlovsk area. The following month the battalion was disbanded. The remnants of the battalion were then incorporated with *Kradschützen* Battalion 23. From 22 April 1943, it was renamed Panzer Reconnaissance *Abteilung* 23.

25th Motorcycle Rifle Battalion

The *Kradschützen* Battalion 25 was formed on 15 November 1940 through the reorganization of the III Battalion of the 40th Infantry Regiment. The battalion was subordinated to the 25th Infantry Division where it was sent to Russia to fight in June 1941. Following heavy losses the Reconnaissance *Abteilung* 25 (motorized) were incorporated into the battalion on 1 May 1942. It was then renamed Panzer Reconnaissance *Abteilung* 125 on 1 April 1943.

26th Motorcycle Rifle Battalion

The *Kradschützen* Battalion 26 was created on 15 September 1942, through the reorganization of the Cycling Battalion 23 of the 23rd Infantry Division. The battalion was subordinated to the 26th Panzer Division. The battalion was deployed with the division to southern France. On 1 April 1943, the battalion was renamed Panzer Reconnaissance *Abteilung* 26.

29th Motorcycle Rifle Battalion

The *Kradschützen* Battalion 29 was formed on 25 February 1941 in Erfurt in Military District XI, from the 4th and 7th companies of the 15th Infantry Regiment and the 2nd and 7th companies of the 71st Infantry Regiment. The battalion was subordinated to the 29th Infantry Division (motorized) and was made up of the 1st-3rd Motorized Rifle Company and the 4th Heavy Company. At the beginning of June 1941, the battalion moved by train to the Warsaw area where it took part in the

Russian campaign from 22 June 1941. From mid-August to early October 1941, the battalion advanced on the Desna area where it successfully fought off strong Russian resistance. The battalion then advanced towards Moscow via Chern–Bogorodisk and Jepifan. In May 1942 it moved to the area south of Orel. Later in the year the battalion then advanced north towards Stalingrad where it was subsequently destroyed in the Battle of Stalingrad in January 1943.

30th Motorcycle Rifle Battalion

The *Kradschützen* Battalion 30 was created on 23 December 1940 in Arnswalde through the reorganization of the III Battalion of the 25th Infantry Regiment. Motorcyclists from the 20th Infantry Division (motorized) and the Reconnaissance *Abteilung* 20 also joined the battalion. The battalion's peacetime location was Arnswalde in Military District II. The battalion was subordinated to the 20th Infantry Division (motorized). In mid-February 1941, the battalion was relocated to France and used as an occupation force in the Auxerre area. In mid-April 1941, the battalion returned to Germany to serve as an OKH reserve for the Balkan campaign. In June 1941 the battalion was sent to Russia. The remnants of Reconnaissance *Abteilung* 20 (motorized) were incorporated into the battalion in 1942. It was then renamed Panzer Reconnaissance *Abteilung* 120 on 29 April 1943.

34th Motorcycle Rifle Battalion

The *Kradschützen* Battalion 34 was formed on 7 January 1941 in Military District XIII. The battalion was subordinated to the 4th Panzer Division. In mid-February 1941, the battalion was sent to France as an occupation force in the area north of Bordeaux. In mid-April 1941 it was relocated to western Hungary as a reserve for the Balkan campaign, in which it no longer took part. From 25 April 1941, the battalion moved into an accommodation area near Poznan before being relocated with the 4th Panzer Division in June 1941. The battalion took part in operations near Moscow in late 1941. After heavy losses in the subsequent defensive battles, the remnants of the 7th Panzer Reconnaissance *Abteilung* were incorporated into the battalion on 5 March 1942. The battalion was deployed in 1942 in the Orel and Bryansk area. In the winter and spring of 1943 it saw heavy fighting in the Kursk area. In April 1943 the battalion was renamed Panzer Reconnaissance *Abteilung* 4.

36th Motorcycle Rifle Battalion

The *Kradschützen* Battalion 36 was created on 9 November 1940 by renaming Machine Gun Battalion 11. The battalion was subordinated to the 36th Infantry Division (motorized). The battalion was sent to the Eastern Front in June 1941 where it suffered high losses. The remnants of Reconnaissance *Abteilung* (motorized) 36 were incorporated into the battalion on 15 March 1942. The battalion was then incorporated into the renamed Division Fusilier Battalion 36 on 1 January 1944.

38th Motorcycle Rifle Battalion

The *Kradschützen* Battalion 38 was formed on 18 November 1940 in Military District VIII. The battalion was subordinated to the 18th Infantry Division. The battalion was sent to Russia in June 1941 where it fought in Army Group Centre and then Army Group North. Following heavy fighting and subsequent losses the remnants of Reconnaissance *Abteilung* (motorized) 18 were incorporated into the battalion on 1 October 1942. On 1 December 1942, the battalion formed a 6th heavy grenade launcher company. In 1943 the battalion was deployed to Lake Ilmen and in April the battalion was renamed Panzer Reconnaissance *Abteilung* 118.

40th Motorcycle Rifle Battalion

The *Kradschützen* Battalion 40 was created on 15 November 1940 from MG Battalion 6. The battalion was subordinated to the 10th Infantry Division (motorized). It fought with the division in Russia from June 1941. On 13 July 1942, remnants of Reconnaissance *Abteilung* 10 (motorized) were incorporated into the battalion. On 1 April 1943, it was reorganized into Panzer Reconnaissance *Abteilung* 110.

43rd Motorcycle Rifle Battalion

The *Kradschützen* Battalion 43 was established in Calbe/Saale, Military District XI, on 2 August 1940. It was subordinated to the 13th Panzer Division. In June 1941 the battalion was sent to Russia where it fought at the Dniepropetrovsk bridgehead. On 10 April 1942, a new *Kradschützen* Battalion 43 was created from the remnants of the battalion and the Panzer Reconnaissance *Abteilung* 13 following high losses. On 3 March 1943, the division reported that the battalion's trench strength was only 100 men following fierce defensive action. In mid-1943 the battalion was renamed Panzer Reconnaissance *Abteilung* 13.

53rd Motorcycle Rifle Battalion

The *Kradschützen* Battalion 53 was formed on 27 October 1941 by *Wehrkreis* III, from the 2nd Battalion of Infantry Regiment 50. The battalion was subordinated to the 3rd Infantry Division (motorized). The battalion was deployed with the division in Russia, and saw action on the central front during its drive on Moscow. At the beginning of 1942 the battalion was re-deployed in the Vjazma area. On 14 March 1942, the remnants of Reconnaissance *Abteilung* 53 (motorized) were incorporated into the battalion. In June 1942 the battalion moved to Army Group South and took part in the German summer offensive towards the Don and Donets. By August 1942 the battalion was embroiled in heavy fighting around Stalingrad where it was subsequently destroyed in January 1943.

54th Motorcycle Rifle Battalion

The *Kradschützen* Battalion 54 was created on 15 October 1940 by reorganizing the 1st Battalion of the 101 Infantry Regiment. The battalion was subordinated to the

14th Infantry Division (motorized). In June 1941 the battalion was sent to the Eastern Front where it fought in Army Group Centre. In 1942, remnants of Reconnaissance *Abteilung* 14 (motorized) were incorporated into the battalion. On 1 April 1943, the battalion was renamed Panzer Reconnaissance *Abteilung* 114.

55th Motorcycle Rifle Battalion

The *Kradschützen* Battalion 55 was established on 9 August 1940 by Military District VIII, by the staff of the 2nd Battalion of the Rifle Regiment 14. The battalion was subordinated to the 5th Panzer Division and was formed into 5 companies. In 1941 the battalion took part in the Balkan campaign. For the invasion of Russia, the battalion was initially left in reserve, but later took part in operations in September 1941 in Army Group Centre. On 24 March 1943 the battalion was renamed Panzer Reconnaissance *Abteilung* 5.

59th Motorcycle Rifle Battalion

The *Kradschützen* Battalion 59 was created on 9 August 1940 by Military District VIII, by the staff of the 2nd Battalion of the 14th Rifle Regiment. The battalion was subordinated to the 9th Panzer Division. On 3 February 1941, the battalion was transported by rail to Romania, from where it was part of the invasion force of Bulgaria in March 1941. During the Balkan campaign, the battalion fought at the Stracin Pass, near Skopljes and Prizrens. In June the battalion was sent to the Eastern Front. The following year it was part of Operation Blue, the German summer offensive towards the Don. Following heavy fighting the battalion was moved to the Gshatsk area, from where it fought in the Rzhev area and then near Shizdra. On 23 March 1943, the battalion was renamed Panzer Reconnaissance *Abteilung* 59.

61st Motorcycle Rifle Battalion

The *Kradschützen* Battalion 61 was formed on 6 August 1940 by *Wehrkreis* IX, from Rifle Regiment 110 and Rifle Regiment 111. The battalion was subordinated to the 11th Panzer Division. The battalion took part in the Balkan campaign in Serbia in 1941 and fought in Army Group South on the Eastern Front from 22 June 1941. In September 1941 it was transferred to Army Group Centre and took part in the German offensive against Moscow. On 1 December 1941, remnants of Panzer Reconnaissance *Abteilung* 231 were incorporated into the battalion. The battalion went on to fight in the Gshatsk area and in the summer of 1942 took part in the German offensive against Don and Donets. The battalion fought around Stalingrad pocket and then saw action in the Kharkov area from February 1943. On 27 April 1943, the battalion was renamed Panzer Reconnaissance *Abteilung* 11.

64th Motorcycle Rifle Battalion

The *Kradschützen* Battalion 64 was created on 16 August 1940 in Military District IV, through the reorganization of Machine Gun Battalion 7. The battalion was subordinated to the 14th Panzer Division. In March 1941 the battalion moved to Hungary and took part in the Balkan campaign. In June 1941 the battalion fought on the Russian southern front. On 1 April 1942, the battalion merged with Panzer Reconnaissance *Abteilung* 40. In the summer of 1942, the battalion took part in the German summer offensive across the Don and Donets towards Stalingrad, where it was destroyed in January 1943.

87th Motorcycle Rifle Battalion

The *Kradschützen* Battalion 87 was established on 9 November 1942 in Norway. The battalion was also known as the *Kradschützen* Battalion 'Rheinberg'. It was subordinated to the 25th Panzer Division in Norway. On 7 April 1943 the battalion was renamed Panzer Reconnaissance *Abteilung* 25.

160th Motorcycle Rifle Battalion

The *Kradschützen* Battalion 160 was formed on 7 August 1940 following the reorganization of Machine Gun Battalion 15. The battalion was subordinated to the 60th Infantry Division. In 1941 the battalion took part in the Balkan campaign. A couple of months later it was sent to the Eastern Front and fought with the Kleist Panzer Group. On 1 April 1942, the battalion merged with Reconnaissance *Abteilung* 160 (motorized). In the summer of 1942, it took part in the German offensive towards Stalingrad, where it was surrounded and destroyed the following winter.

165th Motorcycle Rifle Battalion

The *Kradschützen* Battalion 165 was created on 6 August 1940 in Sennelager, in Military District VI, following the reorganization of MG Battalion 3. The battalion was subordinated to the 16th Infantry Division. The battalion took part in the Balkan campaign with the division in April 1941 and then was transferred to the Eastern Front. On 28 December 1941 it amalgamated with Reconnaissance *Abteilung* 341. On 1 May 1943, the battalion was renamed Panzer Reconnaissance *Abteilung* 116.

345th Motorcycle Rifle Battalion

The *Kradschützen* Battalion 345 was established on 25 November 1942 as a *Kriemhilde* (lance) unit at the Wildflecken military training area. The battalion was subordinated to the 345th Infantry Division (motorized). On 1 March 1943, the battalion was renamed the Panzer Reconnaissance *Abteilung* 29, later 129 as a replacement for the *Kradschützen* Battalion 29 of the 29th Infantry Division (motorized) that was destroyed at Stalingrad.

386th Motorcycle Rifle Battalion

The *Kradschützen* Battalion 386 was formed on 25 November 1942. The battalion was subordinated to the 386th Infantry Division (motorized). On 1 March 1943 it was renamed Panzer Reconnaissance *Abteilung* 53, as a replacement for *Kradschützen* Battalion 53 of the 3rd Infantry Division (motorized) that was destroyed at Stalingrad.

Appendix III

Motorcycle Company, Type b: late 1941 through mid-1942

Kradschützen Company b

1 Officer (K) / Company Commander (Pistol)

Company Headquarters

Headquarters Section

1 NCO / Headquarters Section Leader (SMG)
1 Motor Vehicle NCO (Rifle) (in sidecar)
1 Medic NCO (Pistol) (in sidecar)
1 Messenger / Bugler (Rifle)
4 Motorcycle Messengers (Rifles) (on motorcycles)
2 Motorcyclists (Rifles) (on motorcycles with sidecars)
1 Motor Vehicle Driver (Rifle)
4 motorcycles
2 motorcycles with sidecar
1 car, medium, cross-country (Kfz.15)

Maintenance Section

Senior NCO / Master Mechanic / Section Leader (Pistol) (in sidecar)
1 Motorcyclist / Motor Mechanic (Rifle) (on motorcycle with sidecar)
1 Motor Vehicle Driver / Motor Mechanic (Rifle)
1 Motor Mechanic (Rifle)
1 motorcycle with sidecar
1 maintenance car, light, cross-country (Kfz.2/40)
1 Senior NCO / First Sergeant (Pistol)
1 Senior NCO / Armourer (Pistol)
1 Equipment NCO / Trains Leader (Rifle)
1 NCO / Chief Cook / Motor Vehicle Escort (Rifle)
1 Assistant Armourer / Motor Vehicle Escort (Pistol)
1 Clerk / Motor Vehicle Escort (Rifle) 1 Cook (Rifle)
3 Motor Vehicle Drivers (Rifles)

1 car, medium, cross-country (Kfz.15)
1 truck, light, open, cross-county, for fuel
1 truck, medium, open, cross-county, with field kitchen
Baggage Trains
1 NCO in charge of baggage / clerk (Rifle)
1 Tailor (Rifle)
1 Cobbler / Motor Vehicle Escort (Rifle)
1 Motor Vehicle Driver (Rifle)
1 truck, 3-ton, open, for baggage

3 Rifle Platoons, each with
1 Officer (Z) / Platoon Leader (SMG)
Platoon Headquarters
1 NCO / Platoon Headquarters Leader (Rifle) 1 Messenger / Bugler (Rifle)
1 Motorcycle Messenger (Rifle) (on motorcycle)
2 Motor Vehicle Drivers (Rifles)
1 Stretcher Bearer (Pistol)
1 antitank rifle (7.92mm)
1 motorcycle
2 cars, medium, cross-country (Kfz.15)
3 Rifle Squads, each with
1 NCO Squad Leader (SMG) (in sidecar)
2 MG Gunners (Pistols)
2 Assistant MG Gunners (Pistols)
3 Riflemen (Rifles)
4 Motorcyclists (Rifles) (on motorcycles with sidecars)
2 light machine guns
4 motorcycles with sidecar
1 Heavy Weapons Platoon
1 Officer (Z) / Platoon Leader (SMG)
Platoon Headquarters
1 NCO / Platoon Headquarters Section Leader (Pistol)
1 Messenger (Rifle)
1 Motorcycle Messenger (Rifle) (on motorcycle)
1 Motorcycle Messenger (Rifle) (on motorcycle with sidecar)
2 Motor Vehicle Drivers (Rifles)
1 Stretcher Bearer (Pistol)
1 motorcycle
1 motorcycle with sidecar
2 cars, medium, cross-country (Kfz.15)

2 Heavy Machine Gun Sections, each with
- 1 NCO Section Leader (SMG)
- 2 NCO Gun Team Leaders (Pistols)
- 8 MG Gunners (Pistols)
- 1 Ammunition Handler (Rifle)
- 1 Distance Measurer (Rifle)
- 7 Motorcyclists (Rifles) (on motorcycles with sidecars)
- 1 Motorcyclist (Rifle) (on motorcycle with sidecar for ammo)
- 2 heavy machine guns
- 8 motorcycles with sidecar

1 Mortar Section
- 1 NCO Section Leader (SMG)
- 2 NCO Mortar Team Leaders (Pistols)
- 2 Mortar Gunners (Pistols)
- 2 Assistant Mortar Gunners / Telephone Men (Rifles)
- 4 Ammunition Bearer (Rifles)
- 1 Distance Measurer (Pistol)
- 1 Assistant Armourer (Pistol)
- 3 Motor Vehicle Drivers (Rifles)
- 2 medium mortars (81mm)
- 3 personnel carriers, open, cross-country (Kfz.70)